SO-CWW-398

The Itchy-Scratchy Caterpillar

by Mark Tomblin
illustrated by Doug Jones

SCHOLASTIC INC.

New York • Toronto • London • Auckland
Sydney • Mexico City • New Delhi • Hong Kong

ISBN 978-0-545-24822-8

Copyright © 2010 by Lefty's Editorial Services.

12 11 10 9 8 7 6 5 4 3 2   11 12 13 14 15 16/0

Printed in the U.S.A.   40
First printing, February 2011

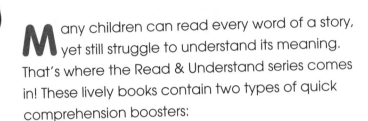

Many children can read every word of a story, yet still struggle to understand its meaning. That's where the Read & Understand series comes in! These lively books contain two types of quick comprehension boosters:

1. **PAGE PROMPTS**—for children to verbally respond to after a page is read

2. **STORY PROMPTS**—for children to verbally respond to after the whole story is read

How do these prompts promote comprehension? When children answer engaging questions about text, their brains are activated to predict, visualize, infer, connect, and more deeply understand a story's meaning. Research shows that teaching kids to "think aloud" about stories helps them develop instant comprehension strategies that they can apply to everything they read.

This special series is also designed to build reading confidence. Toward that end, the stories feature predictable text, highly supportive pictures, and kid-pleasing plots.

Share these super-fun books with children today and they'll read with greater ease and comprehension for years to come!

It was spring. It was sunny. It was the day of the Cooperville Dance Contest. But Darlene Deckler was not happy.

Why do you think Darlene might be unhappy?

Darlene was competing in the contest for the first time. She had never danced in front of a big crowd before. And she was scared. Darlene looked up at the huge stage. Oh no, the show was beginning!

The first person to perform was a girl named Grace. She did a ballet dance. It was really good.

"Wow!" thought Darlene. "I wish I could move like that."

QUESTION

Do you think Darlene believes she can win the dance contest?

A boy named Todd went next. He did a hip-hop dance. It was really, really good.

"Wow!" thought Darlene. "I wish I had moves like that."

The next performers were a sister and brother named Lisa and Larry. They did a tap dance. It was really, really, really good.

"Wow!" thought Darlene. "I wish I had moves like that."

CONNECT

Have you ever performed before a crowd? If not, would you like to?

Darlene was more nervous than ever. How could she compete with such great dancers?

"Maybe I can sneak home," she said to herself.

But it was too late. The announcer called her name.

Look at the picture. What do you see on Darlene's leg?

As Darlene climbed up on the stage, she began to sweat. To make matters worse, something was creeping up her leg. It was an itchy-scratchy caterpillar! Darlene tried to shake it off, but the critter stuck like glue.

Darlene took her place on the stage and the music began. The caterpillar crawled across her knee. *Itchy-scratchy!* Darlene twisted and twirled.

Next, the caterpillar crept up her arm.
Itchy-scratchy! Darlene jumped and jived.
The crowd started to applaud.

QUESTION

Why is Darlene moving in such a crazy way?

After that, the caterpillar inched all the way across her back. *Itchy-scratchy! Itchy-scratchy! Itchy-scratchy!*

Darlene bent and boogied and shook and shimmied and flipped and flopped. The crowd stood on their feet and cheered.

Finally, Darlene was able to grab the tiny creature. She hid it in her hand just in time to take a bow. The crowd went wild!

INFER

Look at Darlene's face. How do you think she feels?

What happened next? The announcer handed Darlene the first-place trophy. Wow! She was the winner of the Cooperville Dance Contest!

"What amazing moves!" he said. "Can you tell us what your dance is called?"

Darlene thought for a moment. Then she peeked in her hand and replied with a laugh, "The Itchy-Scratchy Caterpillar!"

TIE UP

Why did Darlene call her dance "The Itchy-Scratchy Caterpillar"?

Story Prompts

Answer these questions after you have read the book.

1 Can you retell this story in your own words?

2 Is this story silly, serious, or both? Why do you think so?

3 Darlene takes the caterpillar home and puts it in her garden. What happens next? Turn on your imagination and tell a story about it.